Railways & Recollections
The Embsay & Bolton Abbey Steam Railway
Mike Heath

First published in 2019

British Library Cataloguing in Publication Data

A catalogue record for this book is available
from the British Library.

ISBN 978 1 85794 522 5

Silver Link Publishing Ltd
The Trundle
Ringstead Road
Great Addington
Kettering
Northants NN14 4BW

Tel/Fax: 01536 330588
email: sales@nostalgiacollection.com
Website: www.nostalgiacollection.com

Printed and bound in the Czech Republic

Title page: **BOLTON ABBEY** Tne group in this
recently discovered photograph from the turn of
the 19th Century is thought to be the Fowler family
on a day out from Liverpool. The prominent lady
in black at the centre of the group is Rosa Beller
Fowler. Available information indicates that the
young man standing was a member of the family that
founded the Fowler Engineering Company in Leeds.
Courtesy of Stephen Walker, E&BASR

Acknowledgements

The author would like to thank the E&BASR's
Stephen Walker for his assistance and
encouragement with the production of this book
and all the photographers who have kindly allowed
publication of their photographs, mostly from the
Yorkshire Dales Railway Museum Trust Archive.

Front cover: **DRAUGHTON** *Beatrice* pulls away
from the passing loop at Draughton with an Embsay
bound service on 25 May 2017.

Below: **BOLTON ABBEY** On 5 April 2015
Beatrice and Norman, the latter on test following
winter maintenance work, depart with an afternoon
service to Embsay.

Contents

The Skipton and Ilkley railway

Embsay, home of the Embsay & Bolton Abbey Steam Railway, is located just outside the market town of Skipton, 'The Gateway to the Dales'. Marketed as Yorkshire's friendly line, it has one of the finest collections of ex-industrial tank locomotives and working examples operate services over a four mile stretch of the former track bed of the Skipton & Ilkley Railway.

The railways reached Skipton in September 1847 when the Leeds & Bradford (Shipley to Colne extension) Railway arrived from Keighley. The line to Colne was opened the following year. Ilkley was rail connected in August 1865 when the Otley & Ilkley Joint Railway completed its connection with the Leeds & Thirsk Railway, via Otley and Arthington. When first opened Ilkley station was a terminus.

Whilst over the years there had been many proposals to link the two towns it was not until April 1885 that a contract for the construction of the new Skipton & Ilkley Railway was awarded to a company from Bristol, Mousley & Co., and construction commenced two months later. Ilkley station was extended and altered to become a through route and intermediate stations were constructed at Addingham, Bolton Abbey and Embsay. Three years later on the 16th May 1888, the line opened for passenger traffic between Ilkley and Bolton Abbey, Skipton being reached a few months later. Until final closure on 22 March 1965 the line not only provided a local passenger and freight service but also became an important diversionary route whilst track repairs or accident blockage elsewhere were attended to.

SKIPTON The original station, seen here in the 1920s, was opened on 7 September 1847 by the Leeds & Bradford Extension Railway and spent one year as a terminus until the line reached Colne on 2 October 1848. It was relocated slightly north-west of its original location in 1876. Platforms 5 and 6 (inset) were added in 1888 to serve the new route to Ilkley. The station remains open for services from Leeds and onward to Carlisle via the Settle to Carlisle railway and to Lancaster and Morecambe in the west. The buildings have been Grade 2 listed. *YDRMT Archive/YDRMT Archive, David & Charles (inset)*

Right: **EMBSAY** This view looking east was taken on 4 August 1964. The loaded hopper wagons on the shed road were to form a special train to Carlisle, which was due to depart a couple of days later on 6 August. *YDRMT Archive, F.W. Smith*

Below: **EMBSAY** On the last day of local steam passenger workings, 3 January 1959, Stanier 2-6-2T No 40147 arrives at Embsay with a Leeds to Skipton, via Ilkley, train. From 5 January 1959 all local services were taken over by diesel multiple units (DMUs). *YDRMT Archive, F.W. Smith*

Below right: **EMBSAY** Storming through the station on 22 May 1961 is 'Jubilee' Class 4-6-0 No 45571 *South Africa* with a Blackpool to York excursion. *YDRMT Archive, F.W. Smith*

Commencing 5th January 1959

IMPROVED SERVICES at regular intervals **BY DIESEL TRAINS**

LEEDS
BRADFORD
KEIGHLEY
ILKLEY
SKIPTON

EMBSAY 7N54, the Heysham to Tees Yard tanker train, passes through on 4 August 1964. Class 37 D6772 (later No 37702) is in charge. *YDRMT Archive, F.W. Smith*

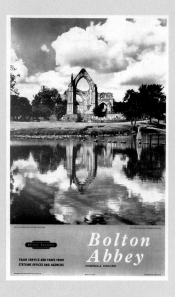

Top left: **BOLTON ABBEY** station in July 1962. *YDRMT Archive, F.W. Smith*

Far left: **BOLTON ABBEY** In this 1958 photograph Class 4 2-6-4T No 42093 has just stopped with a Bradford Forster Square to Skipton train. Note the Porter checking tickets before passengers climb the footbridge steps. By the far bench against the main station building is the roller used to roll the stone chipping surface of the platform. *YDRMT Archive, F.W. Smith*

BOLTON ABBEY On Sunday 19 June 1960 a Class 108 two-car Derby-built DMU is heading back to Leeds; at that time on summer Sundays all DMU services turned back at Bolton Abbey. The main station platform once extended beyond the signal box, the rotting boards at the base clearly showing where it use to be! *YDRMT Archive, P. Sunderland, F.W. Smith collection*

DIESEL TRAIN SERVICE
FROM
BOLTON ABBEY
and ILKLEY

Sundays 21st June to 6th September 1964
inclusive

ADDINGHAM Thought to date from circa 1954, this photograph depicts Stanier Class 3 2-6-2T No 40117 arriving at Addingham. Note the signal box, goods yard and shed behind the locomotive. *YDRMT Archive, F.W. Smith*

ADDINGHAM Opened in 1888, the station boasted two platforms, a signal box, goods shed, yard and cattle dock. Today very little evidence of it exists as the area has become a residential estate. These two photographs date from 1966, just after closure. *YDRMT Archive*

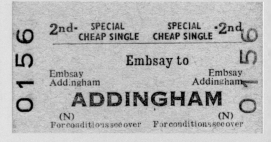

Left: **ILKLEY** When first opened in August 1865, Ilkley station was the western terminus of the Otley & Ilkley Joint Railway. The arrival of the line from Skipton in 1888 saw the station assume the status of a junction with through Platforms 3 and 4 serving the new route. Although the Skipton line closed in 1965, the tracks were only lifted in 1983 and the platforms infilled during electrification work in the 1990s, the area becoming a car park. This photograph dates from 1966, just after closure. *YDRMT Archive*

Below left: **ILKLEY** On leaving the station trains heading for Skipton passed over Brook Street Bridge. With a volcanic exhaust 'Patriot' 4-6-0 No 45505 *The Royal Army Ordnance Corps* heads a returning excursion to Whaley Bridge on 15 May 1955. *YDRMT Archive, F. W. Smith*

Left: **ILKLEY** With the station in the distance ex-L&YR Class 2P 2-4-2T No 10671 is captured leaving with a Leeds to Skipton, via Ilkley, working in 1948. *YDRMT Archive, F. W. Smith*

The Preservation Society

Closure of the line excluded the Skipton to Grassington & Threshfield branch and, while track-lifting soon commenced, the section between Embsay and the junction with the Grassington branch, just east of the station, was also left intact for stone traffic from the Skipton Rock Company.

In the late 1960s closure of the Skipton to Grassington line was strongly rumoured. Local railway enthusiasts, encouraged by the success of the volunteers in preserving the Middleton and Keighley & Worth Valley railways, sought to save this branch line and in 1965 set up the Embsay & Grassington Railway Preservation Society, based at Embsay.

However, soon afterwards British Rail revealed that far from being closed, the line was to be maintained as far as Swinden Quarry at Cracoe where the works had been taken over by Tilcon Ltd. It was planned to introduce a regular flow of stone trains and this mineral traffic has continued to this day.

As a result, the preservationists revised their plans to the opening of a steam railway centre based around Embsay station and the small section of track that remained. The society changed its name to the Yorkshire Dales Railway Society (YDRS) to reflect this new proposal.

BOLTON ABBEY These photographs show track-lifting in progress around Bolton Abbey station.
Both YDRMT Archive, Dave Cash

The early years of preservation

In 1970, following agreement with British Rail, the YDRS commenced the renting of Embsay station, giving it a base from which it could operate. From the beginning society members had concluded that the most economic way of running and maintaining a fleet of steam locomotives was to use former industrial types, which at the time were readily available and would offer lower running costs than ex-British Railways main-line locos. Notwithstanding this decision, visitors at the time would have seen 8F 2-8-0 No 48151 in the sidings. Now owned by West Coast Railways at Carnforth and a regular on main-line steam specials, the ex-BR locomotive was stored at Embsay for five years prior to its restoration.

The first locomotive to arrive at Embsay was the oil-burning Hudswell Clarke 0-4-0ST *Nellie*. Having spent much of its working life at the Esholt Sewage Works near Bradford, it returned to that city, in 1974, for display at its Industrial Museum.

As the number of locomotives in its fleet increased, the society held traction engine rallies and open days, offering brake van rides to raise funds for its project. The arrival of two former electric multiple unit coaches in 1972, transferred to Yorkshire from the Altrincham Electric Railway Society, allowed the society to add proper passenger services to its money-raising activities.

Ex-British Railways 8F No 48151.

An early traction engine rally.

0-4-0ST *Nellie*.

The former electric multiple unit coaches behind *Slough Estates Ltd No 5. All YDRMT Archive, Charles Adams*

Left and below left: The society's second locomotive was the 1925-built Avonside 0-4-0ST *Fred*, seen here at Embsay working push-pull services with *Chemicals*, a 1924-built Barclay 0-4-0ST. *Chemicals* later went to work in the Shipley scrap iron works, while *Fred* headed overseas to a steam centre in Belgium. *YDRMT Archive, Gordon Findlay and Dave Cash*

Right: The pair approach Bow Bridge Junction. *YDRMT Archive, Charles Adams*

Below: Hudswell Clarke 0-6-0ST *Slough Estates Ltd No 5* arrived at Embsay in working order in 1973. A few years later it became first locomotive to be overhauled at Embsay. *YDRMT Archive, Charles Adams*

The fact that the coaches were air-braked meant that they were not compatible with steam vacuum brakes, necessitating a locomotive at either end of the train – not the most economic way of running services, but it enabled the society to raise revenue. Push-pull services continued until British Railways imposed a ban on all preservation societies operating services on track leased from it, citing insurance problems.

A Light Railway Order would be required to allow services to resume and an application was therefore submitted. The list of works that was prepared by the Inspector was extensive and included the construction of a run-round loop at Bow Bridge Junction. Steam trains were not able to recommence until May 1979.

Above: Peckett 0-4-0ST *Foleshill* dated from 1948, and is seen here on push-pull duties with the Hudswell Clarke 0-6-0ST *Slough Estates Ltd No 5. Foleshill* is now based at a steam museum on the island of Jersey.

Abovet: During the British Railways ban, the only steam train operation was provided by the 9½-inch-gauge 2-4-2 locomotive *King Tut*, which ran steam-hauled train rides on track laid across the car park.

Right: The reopening train. *All YDRMT Archive, Charles Adams*

Steam trains to Bolton Abbey

With the society now established at a 'reopened' Embsay station, attention turned to the disused track bed towards Bolton Abbey. It was decided that the extension would be constructed in stages as funds and labour permitted, and the society's name was changed to the Embsay Steam Railway to more accurately reflect its location.

In 1982 the first mile, to a run-round loop at Skibeden, was completed. Five years later trains ran on a further half-mile to Holywell Halt, where a new 'station' was built.

Just beyond the Halt was Holywell Bridge, which carried the main A59 road over the railway. This was a major obstacle to further progress as the local authority, in response to concerns about the structure, had filled in the cutting and below the bridge to strengthen it. The major reinforcement works to overcome this problem included the introduction of a steel tunnel under the bridge.

The society intended the next stage to be to a run-round loop at Draughton, but local opposition resulted in planning permission being refused and the railway relocating its proposed loop to Stoneacre. This section opened in 1991.

Abovet: This is Holywell bridge in 1966, just after the line closed and before the local authority filled in the cutting. *YDRMT Archive*

Left: The bridge today, showing the tunnel lining and Holywell Halt beyond.

EMBSAY CRAG   BOLTON ABBEY

**EMBSAY & BOLTON ABBEY
STEAM RAILWAY**

STEAM TRAINS EVERY SUNDAY   SUMMER SERVICES UP TO 5 DAYS A WEEK
TALKING TIMETABLE TEL (01756) 795189 GENERAL ENQUIRIES TEL (01756) 794727

Illustrated guide available free from:
The Publicity Manager, Bolton Abbey Station, Bolton Abbey, Skipton, North Yorkshire. BD23 6AF

This page: Railway operations to Stoneacre were very successful and gave the impetus to the purchase of the remaining trackbed to Bolton Abbey. There then followed a period of extensive works that included the clearance of undergrowth, renewal of culverts and drains, repairs to fencing, and the construction of three new bridges. The loop at Stoneacre was slightly extended, a signal box installed and signalling altered to control what was now a passing loop. After arrival at Bolton Abbey, the title of Embsay & Bolton Abbey Steam Railway adopted by the society. *All YDRMT Archive, Charles Adams*

Left: The first works train steamed into Bolton Abbey in February 1997. *YDRMT Archive, M. G. Riley*

While the track-laying gang made their way towards them, the team working at the site of Bolton Abbey station were also toiling away. The original building had become a derelict shell and had to be demolished. A complete rebuild was necessary and it was agreed that the basis for the design for the new building would be the original 1888 plans.

The construction project involved many bodies. At the time the local Yorkshire Television schedules included a programme called *Action Time* and included appeals for labour and materials to complete local construction projects. The Bolton Abbey scheme was one to benefit, and a local firm of architects became involved, drawing up all the necessary plans. Offers of materials flooded in and a full electrical installation was also secured. The construction itself was carried out under the supervision of Sir Robert McAlpine and all told more than 170 businesses contributed to the project between 1995 and 1997.

The opening of Bolton Abbey took place on 26 October 1997 with Sir Robert McAlpine as guest of honour. The official opening took place on 1 May 1998 with Sir William McAlpine headlining the event.

Photos depicting the 'before and after' stages of the station's rebuilding. *YDRMT Archive, R. Milner and F. W. Smith*

Below: The 'big day'. *Both YDRMT Archive, M. G. Riley*

Left, below left and above: While the station was under construction the signalling department was working on a signal box recovered from Guiseley station, where it had become redundant. The box had to be moved in two sections and was re-erected at the Embsay end of the platform. *YDRMT Archive, J. Furness and F. W. Smith*

Top right: The water column that now serves locomotives at Bolton Abbey came from Skipton station. Here it is seen in the process of being removed under the gaze of a crowd of onlookers. *YDRMT Archive, J. Furness*

Centre right: After restoration at Embsay the water column was hauled to Bolton Abbey behind *Primrose*, and is seen here about to be craned into position. *YDRMT Archive, M. Warner*

Right: The station is almost ready to receive passenger trains. Track and watering services are in place with final preparation work being undertaken around station itself. *YDRMT Archive, M. G. Riley*

Embsay station past and present

Above and above right: The station is seen first from the footbridge on 18 May 1958. In today's view the waiting shelter and platform canopy represent the most obvious changes. *YDRMT Archive, F.W. Smith/author*

Left and right: The 'past' view looking east was taken on 4 August 1964, and the equivalent in January 2017. *YDRMT Archive, F.W. Smith/author*

Above left and above: Embsay station is just after closure in 1966, and again in 2017. *YDRMT Archive/author*

Left: The most notable additions to the station are these two beautifully restored buildings. The ex-Midland Railway cabman's shelter was brought in from Ilkley and for a few years served as a ticket office until a former booking office from Barmouth in Wales was brought in and refurbished. The cabman's hut then reverted to a waiting shelter.

Bolton Abbey station past and present

The station is seen first in the 1930s, with the large iron water tower and the water columns it served visible in the background. These were removed in the 1950s.

The 1964 view shows the precast-concrete-edged platforms that replaced the original wooden structure in the late 1940s.

As there is no footbridge (currently), the comparative 2017 photograph was taken from platform level. *YDRMT Archive, Douglas Thompson, F. W. Smith collection/YDRMT Archive, F. W. Smith/author*

Bolton Abbey station is seen here in 1966 and 2017. The Society is aiming to complete Platform 2 with an access footbridge and associated station buildings. Progress has already been made – one of the walls is now complete and work is under way to complete the rest of the structure.

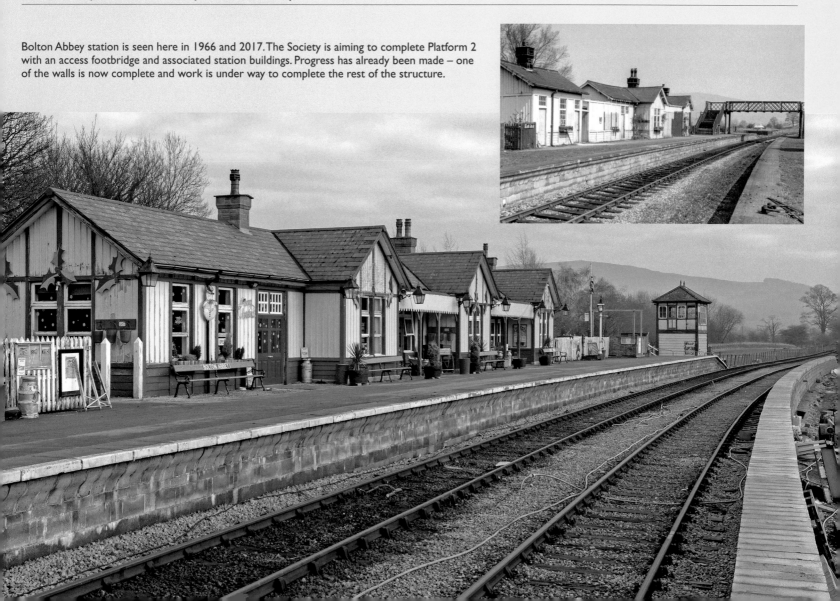

Locomotives

As mentioned previously, in the early days of preservation the society had decided to purchase former industrial locomotives to operate the services. All the locomotives in the extensive collection have at some stage in their life been employed on industrial railways and include many examples built in Yorkshire.

Examples of locomotives stored awaiting or undergoing overhaul

At present some locomotives are stored awaiting overhaul and these, together with those undergoing overhaul, are not currently on display to the public, but are illustrated in the following photographs.

York No 1 Built by the Yorkshire Engine Company in 1949, this 0-4-0ST worked for the National Coal Board at South Kirkby Colliery near Barnsley. It was an early arrival on the railway and this photograph dates from around 1975. *YDRMT Archive, Charles Adams*

South Hetton No 69 This Austerity 0-6-0ST was built by Hunslet in 1953 and arrived on the railway from NCB South Hetton Colliery in County Durham. It was withdrawn from service in 1984. This photograph is thought to have been taken shortly after its arrival. *YDRMT Archive, C. Boylan*

Warspite (formerly No 8 Sir Robert Peel) Another product of the Hunslet works, No 8 dates from 1952 and has travelled widely in both its working and preserved life. It was delivered to NCB Baggeridge Colliery near Walsall, then moved to Hilton Main Colliery, Granville Colliery, Cannock Wood Colliery, West Cannock Colliery and finally Bickershaw Colliery in Leigh. In preservation it has spent time on the East Lancashire Railway, the Gloucestershire Warwickshire Railway and the Chinnor & Princes Risborough Railway. It arrived at Embsay in December 2000, and is seen here crossing Summerseat Viaduct on the East Lancashire Railway in 1989.

No 140 This PLA 0-6-0T was built by Hudswell Clarke in 1948 and initially worked at NCB Horden Colliery, County Durham. The black & white photo shows the loco at Thrislington Colliery in 1968, two years before it arrived at Embsay. On 6 October 2007 it was photographed on a vintage train. *YDRMT Archive (b&w photo)*

Thomas (formerly Dorothy)
This Hudswell Clarke 0-6-0ST, built in 1922, arrived on the railway in the 1970s, as seen in the first picture, having worked at British Steel, Scunthorpe. Its poor condition meant that it spent a number of years in the sidings before restoration commenced. Again, its condition resulted in it being chosen for conversion to create the railway's own 'Thomas the Tank Engine', as seen in the May 2007 photograph. *YDRMT Archive, Charles Adams*

Monkton No 1 Built in Leeds by Hunslet in 1953, this Austerity 0-6-0ST was delivered new to Monkton Colliery at Royston near Barnsley. On the closure of that pit, in 1967, it moved to North Gawber Colliery, Mapplewell, just north of Barnsley. It came to Embsay in 1980 and was used during the first 'Harvest of Steam' weekend. Sidelined for a number of years after initial withdrawal,

it was not until 1997 that its overhaul started. It is seen here in the sidings at Embsay shortly after its arrival on the railway. *YDRMT Archive, Charles Adams*

Above right: Returning to traffic in 2002, *Monkton No 1* was photographed on a freight working on 20 September 2008, before problems first noted in 2006 caused early withdrawal for another overhaul.

Slough Estates Ltd No 5 A 1939-built Hudswell Clarke 0-6-0ST, it was destined for the Slough Trading Estate in Buckinghamshire, where it worked until the mid-1970s. It was bought and moved to Embsay in working condition (see the photograph on page 11). While it is currently awaiting its third overhaul, these photos show it during its first overhaul and being tested on its completion when it became the first loco overhauled on the railway. *YDRMT Archive, Charles Adams*

No S134 *Wheldale* is a standard Austerity locomotive, built in 1944 by Hunslet of Leeds. Although it is referred to by its NCB number, S134, it first became part of the Army's fleet, based at Bicester, as No 134. It came to the railway from NCB Wheldale Colliery, Castleford, where it was photographed, remaining at work until the early 1980s. *Wheldale* arrived at the railway in good mechanical condition, and was returned to service for a ten-year spell, during which it became one of the main members of the fleet. *YDRMT Archive, John Furness*

Below left: On 12 September 1993 *Wheldale* makes an explosive departure from Embsay.

Below: Wheldale's boiler certificate expired midway through the 1990s, and a sad, forlorn-looking locomotive is seen at Bolton Abbey station. A huge fundraising effort is under way to finance the locomotive's restoration. The cost will be substantial – well in excess of £200,000 – and that's using the railway's own volunteers! At the end of 2018 they had raised £130,000 and now hope to commence restoration work during 2019.

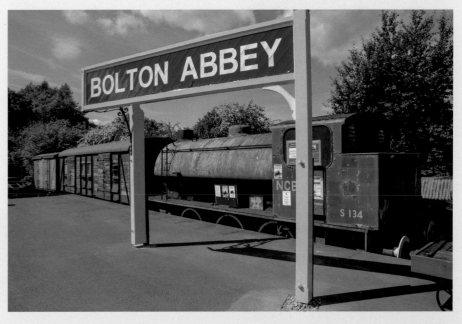

No S121 *Primrose No 2* was one of the earliest arrivals on the line and for many years was one of the main engines on the railway. It had worked for the NCB at Peckfield Colliery, Micklefield, having been built in Leeds by Hunslet in 1952. It was initially overhauled in the late 1980s and worked the line before a crack in the firebox saw it again withdrawn in 1999. While work is in progress, there is no date set for completion. The first picture shows *Primrose* at Peckfield just before leaving for Embsay, and the second arriving at Embsay, with a service train, on 21 June 1998. *YDRMT Archive, Charles Adams*

Above: **No 22** This 0-4-0ST is a product of the Andrew Barclay works in Kilmarnock, emerging in 1952. It worked at East Hetton Colliery, where it carried its red livery, and was later employed at the Fishburn Coke Works. It is seen here alongside *Slough Estates Ltd No 5* at Embsay shortly after it had arrived on the railway. *YDRMT Archive, Charles Adams*

Left: No 22 arrives at Embsay on 20 September 1992.

Above: Photographed on 11 September 1994, No 22 is in the black livery of Fishburn Coke Works. The locomotive has been out of service since 2000, but work is progressing on its restoration.

Right: **Annie** When Yates Duxbury Ltd's paper mill opened near Bury in 1908 it required locomotives for its railway system. An order was placed with Bristol-based Peckett & Sons, and this 0-4-0ST, named *Annie*, was the first to arrive and spent all its working life at the mill. Withdrawn in 1970, *Annie* initially went to the Bury Transport Museum, but it was unable to carry out restoration work and was about to scrap the loco. A YDR member stepped in with the intention of placing *Annie* on a plinth behind Embsay station, but this proposal fell through due to the loco's poor condition. *Annie* is seen at the paper mill in 1967.
YDRMT Archive, R. Monk

Top right: In 1984 *Annie* was purchased by John Furness, and is seen in poor condition on arrival at the railway.
YDRMT Archive

Right: John proceeded to oversee *Annie*'s overhaul and after many years' service hauling vintage trains her boiler certificate finally expired in February 2003 and a further overhaul commenced. Here she heads a vintage train on 12 September 1993.

Locomotives in recent service

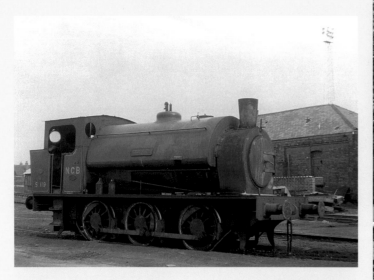

Above left: **Beatrice** This 0-6-0ST was built by Hunslet in 1945 and worked at Acton Hall Colliery, Pontefract. *YDRMT Archive, John Furness*

Left: Beatrice proved to be a strong and popular engine but had to be withdrawn for overhaul before the railway reached Bolton Abbey. She is seen here in service alongside *Annie* on 12 September 1993.

Above: Beatrice re-emerged from the works in 2013 and has been a regular in service ever since. She was photographed at Embsay on 23 May 2017.

Below: **Norman** This 0-6-0ST 'Austerity' locomotive is owned by Southern Locomotives Limited, based on the South Coast at Swanage. It was built by Robert Stephenson's Locomotive Works in 1943 and, as No WD5050, was delivered to 154 Railway Operating Company at Long Marston on 24 April of that year in khaki livery, in readiness for the D-Day landings. In August 1944 it was moved to the Longmoor Military Railway and was renumbered 75050. In December 1944 it was shipped to France and travelled to the SNCB depot at Antwerp Dam. Utilised for local services over the next six months, it was transferred in May 1945 to 155 Railway Workshops Company for wheel-turning before returning to Antwerp. On 19 February 1946 it was returned to the UK and bought by Doncaster Amalgamated Colliery Ltd. It

remained there, or close by, for 24 years until it was moved to Askern Main Colliery in 1970.

Initial restoration was carried out at the Midland Railway Centre, before the loco was moved to Sellinge, then to Swanage in June 2009. In October 2010, midway through its overhaul, *Norman* moved to Embsay and was completed in the railway's workshops, entering traffic in time for the 2011 season. On 21 May of that year *Norman*, in basic green livery, departs from Bolton Abbey.

Above: Four years later, on 4 May 2015, the locomotive passes Holywell Halt carrying the black livery of NCB No 2 Area Durham and the number 69.

Illingworth/Mitchell This Hudswell Clarke 0-6-0ST was built in 1916 and used for war work at the Ministry of Munitions at Gretna Green. Bradford Corporation bought it in 1922 to work trains over the Nidd Valley Light Railway between Pateley Bridge and Lofthouse and up to Scar House reservoir. At that time it carried the name *Mitchell*, but in 1930 this was changed to *Illingworth*. When the line closed in 1936 it was sold to Sir Robert McAlpine Ltd, where it carried the name *Harold* and worked on the company's Ebbw Vale steelworks project. Ownership passed to Mowlem in 1940 and once again the locomotive was called upon for war duties at Swynnerton and Ruddington, now taking the name *Swynnerton*. Before it was consigned for scrap in 1957 there was a period of work on Workington's breakwater construction and Mowlem's Braehead power station construction.

Somehow the engine survived intact, spending half its life as a rusting hulk, passing through several owners but never on public display. Stephen Middleton, owner of 'Stately Trains', which operates on the railway, was surprised to discover that an ex-Nidd Valley Light Railway locomotive, a railway once local to him and long since closed, had survived. *Illingham* was found at Great Fransham station near Swaffham in Norfolk and its purchase negotiated; it is seen here (top left) in 'as found' condition *Stephen Middleton, 'Stately Trains'*

Restoration took many years, and the locomotive was tested on shuttle services in 2017, as seen here (top right) in May, carrying the *Illingworth* name on one side and *Mitchell* on the other. It is expected to enter full service in early 2019. *Stephen Middleton, 'Stately Trains'*

Right: **GWR 0-6-2T No 5643** is a roving ambassador for the Furness Railway Trust, but is currently based on the Yorkshire railway. It emerged from Swindon Works in October 1925 and spent its working life in and around South Wales before withdrawal in 1963. Originally purchased for a now defunct preservation project in South Wales, it was soon transferred to Lancashire and was based at the now closed Steamtown Railway Museum at Carnforth. In 1986 it was purchased by members of the Lakeside Railway Society and moved to their Haverthwaite base three years later. The LRS evolved into the Furness Railway Trust, with ownership of the locomotive transferred accordingly. Restoration was completed in 2006. Here No 5643 works away from the passing loop at Draughton towards Embsay on 6 December 2009. *Karl Heath*

Left and below left: **Taff Vale tank No 85** Another long-term visitor, which also hails from South Wales, is the Keighley & Worth Valley Railway's Taff Vale tank. No 85 was built in 1899 for the Taff Vale Railway, which connected the Cardiff area with the coal-mining industry located to the north. The TVR was taken over by the Great Western Railway in 1922. Surplus to requirements in 1927, the engine was withdrawn and two years later was sold to the Lambton, Hetton & Joicey Colliery, where it worked through nationalisation until withdrawal in 1968. It arrived on the Keighley & Worth Valley Railway in December 1970.

In the 1990s it was rebuilt to its original outline by Worth Valley volunteers and gave good service until withdrawal in 2010. TVR No 85 then entered the workshops at Haworth and re-entered service in its original fully lined-out Taff Vale Railway livery in 2016.

Visiting tender locomotives

The railway has often called upon the services of
tank locomotives from other preserved railways to
supplement its own fleet in keeping with its policy
of employing former industrial tank locomotives
to operate services. However, over the years there
have been a number of former main-line tender
locomotives visiting the line for special events.

The first tender engine to haul trains on the line in
the preservation era was former London Midland &
Scottish Class 4F No 4422, when in 1993 it visited
from its then home at the North Staffordshire
Railway (now known as the Churnet Valley Railway).
Its current base is the West Somerset Railway. On 12
September 1993 No 4422 was photographed at the
head of a freight train due to depart from Embsay
station.

The North Eastern Railway 'J27' Class 0-6-0s were
designed for freight work in the North East of
England. Carrying the British Railways number that it
was given following nationalisation of the railways in
1948, No 65894 visited the line in 1998 and is seen
hauling a train of hoppers away from Bolton Abbey
on 21 June. The locomotive is owned by the North
Eastern Locomotive Preservation Group (NELPG),
based on the North Yorkshire Moors Railway.

One of the oldest, and most regular, visitors is former Lancashire & Yorkshire Railway 'A' Class/Class '27' No 1300 (LMS No 12322, BR No 52322). This vintage locomotive dates from 1895 when it emerged from the L&YR's Horwich Works. The photograph dates from 12 July 2014 and was taken just before the line passes beneath the Prior's Lane road bridge. *Karl Heath*

A visitor from the Great Central Railway was BR Standard 2 Class 2 2-6-0 No 78019. On 26 September 2009 it makes a powerful departure from Bolton Abbey in charge of the Vintage Train comprising carriages belonging to 'Stately Trains'.

In 2008, in what was a coup for the railway, LNER Class 'D49/1' No 246 *Morayshire* (built in 1928) made its first foray outside Scotland to visit a preserved line south of the border. On 21 September it was working passenger services and is captured having just left Holywell Halt for Embsay. *Karl Heath*

The 1988 Centenary

To celebrate the railway's centenary in 1988 two locomotives were hired in. The first was '|72' Class No 69023 *Joem*, owned by the North Eastern Locomotive Preservation Group (NELPG). The design of this locomotive dates back to 1898 when the North Eastern Railway constructed the first of the class. *Joem* was one of the last built at Darlington in 1951.

The second visitor was the 0-6-0WT (Well Tank) *Bellerophon*, which was built for the Haydock Collieries, Lancashire, in 1874. Its owner is the Vintage Carriages Trust, based at Ingrow on the Keighley & Worth Valley Railway.

Locomotives from the 'home' fleet that operated during the centenary year included No 22, *Slough Estates Ltd No 5*, and *Beatrice*.

On 30 October 1988 the railway held a 'Hallowe'en' event with children encouraged to dress as wizards and warlocks. *Bellerophon* became a 'wizard' for the day!

HARVEST OF STEAM WEEKEND

For many years the railway's annual enthusiast event was called the 'Harvest of Steam', when all available locomotives were called upon to operate an intensive timetable of services. For the 2002 event *Monkton No 1*, *Cranford No 2*, *Annie* and a long-term visitor from the East Somerset Railway, No 68005, were all in steam.

Above: 0-6-0ST No 68005 was never actually a British Railways locomotive, notwithstanding the livery carried here. It was built as a standard 'Austerity' locomotive by Stephenson & Hawthorn in 1945 and was acquired by the East Somerset Railway from the NCB's Swalwell Colliery in Durham. The ESR converted the saddle tank to resemble a British Railways version.

Left: Annie with a vintage train

Above: For the event the railway assembled a large loose-coupled goods train, which ran up and down the line all weekend. Here *Cranford No 2* heads the freight between Holywell Halt and Embsay.

Left: For the return trip to Bolton Abbey *Monkton No 1* was added to the ensemble.

STATELY TRAINS

The railway often uses the Edwardian and Victorian wooden-bodied carriages that belong to the 'Stately Trains' fleet, owned by Stephen Middleton; at quieter times of the year it runs them instead of the standard Mark 1s. During the summer vintage trains are run on two-train days and for the 'Dining Special' services.

Right: At the rear of this train is **GER No 14**, built by the Great Eastern Railway in 1889 to haul VIPs over the GER system. It survived as a passenger coach, and also ran on Sir William McAlpine's private railway before being fully restored as part of the 'Stately Trains' fleet.

Next is **GNoSR No 34**, built in 1896 for use by the Great North of Scotland Railway. Although it underwent several major rebuilds during its life, it has been restored to being a 1st/3rd six-wheeled carriage, and impressive it most certainly is! It is also thought to be the only Scottish coach operating in England.

Then comes **No 37**, also built as a saloon by the GER in 1897, and reputed to have been the private saloon of Princess Alice, as it has several interior features (discovered during restoration) that a 3rd Class saloon would not include.

Next to the engine is **L&Y No 1**, built in 1906 for the Lancashire & Yorkshire Railway's Directors. It was rebuilt by both the LMS and BR, but has been restored by Stephen Middleton to its original condition.
Stephen Middleton, 'Stately Trains'

Far right and right: The latest addition to the fleet is London & South Western Railway 1st Open Royal Saloon No 17, built for Queen Victoria in 1887. Its restoration was filmed by Channel 4 and was the subject of one episode of its five-part documentary series that put into sharp focus the craftsman's art of vintage carriage restoration.
Stephen Middleton, 'Stately Trains'/ Author

Right: On 5 October 2013 0-6-0ST *Sir Berkeley*, which itself dates from 1890, was visiting from the Middleton Railway, Leeds, and formed a truly vintage train, seen here pulling away from the loop at Draughton.

Below: Lancashire & Yorkshire Railway 'A' Class/Class '27' No 1300 (LMS No 12322, BR No 52322), built in 1895, creates another vintage image on 4 May 2014 as it heads away from Holywell Halt.

Wartíme weekend

Once a year, over a weekend, the railway steps back to the difficult times of 1942-43 wartime Britain. Over both days the stations are set back in time and various re-enactment societies attend on both days. Visitors are encouraged to watch out for the Home Guard, soldiers and airmen returning home on leave, the long-suffering civilians and, of course, the spivs! There are also displays of military vehicles at each station.

A journey along the line today

EMBSAY & BOLTON ABBEY

STEAM RAILWAY

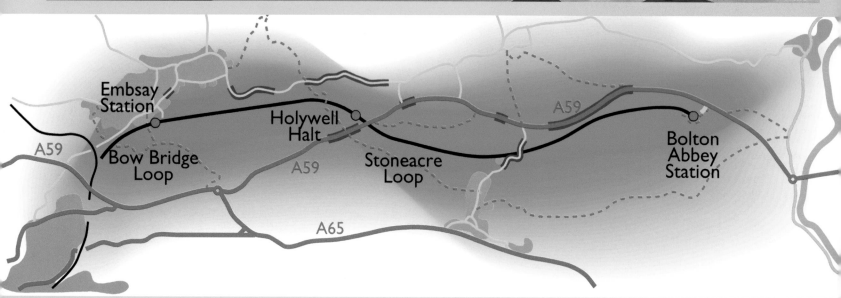

Embsay
Station

Bow Bridge
Loop

Holywell
Halt

Stoneacre
Loop

A59

A59

A65

Bolton
Abbey
Station

A59

Bolton Abbey station

MIDLAND RAILWAY.

7 VICT. CAP. 18 SEC. 238 ENACTS "THAT IF ANY "PERSON SHALL BE OR TRAVEL OR PASS UPON FOOT "UPON THE MIDLAND RAILWAY WITHOUT THE "LICENSE AND CONSENT OF THE MIDLAND RAILWAY "COMPANY, EVERY PERSON SO OFFENDING SHALL "FORFEIT AND PAY ANY SUM NOT EXCEEDING TEN "POUNDS FOR EVERY SUCH OFFENCE." NOTICE IS THEREFORE HEREBY GIVEN THAT ALL PERSONS FOUND TRESPASSING UPON THIS RAILWAY OR THE WORKS THEREOF WILL BE PROSECUTED.

JUNE 1906.   ALEXIS L. CHARLES.
                                         SECRETARY.

BOLTON ABBEY STATION is sited in one of the most beautiful parts of Yorkshire and the railway's volunteers have lovingly recreated it in the original Midland Railway style of the 1800s. The main platform and the station buildings were reopened in 1998, and recently a former Midland Railway signal box has been purchased and placed in the location of the original, at the east end of Platform 1. Opposite Platform 1 the next phase of development, the reinstatement of Platforms 2 and 3, is under way. Eventually there will be additional station buildings and a footbridge to connect the platforms.

Right: **DRAUGHTON**
The Dales in all their autumnal splendour: this November 2013 photograph was taken from the edge of the village of Draughton and shows the train emerging from the woods that surround Hambleton Quarry.
Karl Heath

Below: **BOLTON ABBEY** On 5 April 2015 *Beatrice* is about to depart with an afternoon service to Embsay.

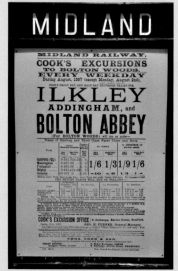

Above: **DRAUGHTON** During the Branch Line Weekend in May 2014 *Norman* approaches Draughton with a mixed goods train.

Above: The Dales as a winter wonderland: *Norman* heads a passenger service on 15 January 2012. *Karl Heath*

Left: **PRIORS LANE** Three years earlier, on 19 December 2009, the 'Santa Specials' were in the capable hands of GWR No 5643. This pre-Christmas train is about to pass beneath the Priors Lane road bridge. *Karl Heath*

Left: **DRAUGHTON** The siding at Draughton has road access from Priors Lane and is used to transfer stock to and from road transport. This includes the exchange of locomotives between heritage railways. On 18 April 2017, as *Norman*, now in NCB livery, passes by, GWR tank No 5643 is being hauled on to a low-loader heading for a Gala event on the North Norfolk Railway.

Above: **DRAUGHTON** At the same location in August 2010 we see Hunslet-built 'Austerity' Class 0-6-ST No 22, built in Leeds in 1956 for NCB Graig Merthyr Colliery in South Wales. It was paying a flying visit to the Yorkshire line from its base at the Nene Valley Railway near Peterborough.

PRIORS LANE This panoramic view has the Priors Lane road bridge in the foreground and the passing loop and signal box at Draughton in the middle background. In between, *Norman* and its short freight train have just exited the loop heading towards Bolton Abbey.

Above: **DRAUGHTON** On a wintry December day in 2017 the Taff Vale tank pilots *Norman* away from the passing loop with a 'Santa Special'.

Top right: **DRAUGHTON** This stretch of the line between the loop and the A59 road bridge is one of the most accessible and is the most photographed section as Embsay-bound trains pull away from the loop. In this 2008 view two 'Santa Specials' have just passed each other.

Right: **DRAUGHTON** For the 2008 'Santa' season GWR 0-6-0PT No 6435 was hired in from the Bodmin & Wenford Railway in Cornwall.

Above: **DRAUGHTON** On 5 December 2010 another 'visitor' is on 'Santa' duty. *Darfield* is another product of the Hunslet Engine Company of Leeds, emerging in 1953. It is named after the colliery at which it worked. In preservation Embsay was its home from 1975 until it was transferred to the Llangollen Railway in 1988. It returned to Yorkshire as a visitor in June 2008 and saw regular service until it headed back to Wales after the 2010 Christmas services. It is currently at the Chasewater Railway carrying the name *Holly Bank No 3.*

Right: **DRAUGHTON** For a short period at the back end of 2012 the railway had a shortage of its own motive power to fulfil its timetable. An arrangement with the Kent & East Sussex Railway saw 'USA' 0-6-0T No 65 head north to ease the situation. These interesting locomotives were built between 1942 and 1943 by the United States Army Transportation Corps and a number were purchased and adapted by the Southern Railway after the end of the Second World War to replace the old London & South Western Railway 'B4' Class locos that worked the docks at Southampton.

Above: **DRAUGHTON** Another Furness Railway Trust locomotive currently on hire to the railway is the former War Department 'Austerity' 0-6-0ST *Cumbria*. On New Year's Day 2019 it is seen in a typical Yorkshire Dales railway landscape.

Left: **DRAUGHTON** On 4 May 2015 another visitor for that year's Branch Line Gala was NCB Backworth No 47 *Moorbarrow*, built by Robert Stephenson & Hawthorn in 1955, was in charge of a demonstration freight working.

DRAUGHTON The final photograph from this section of the line sees the 'Taffy' tank in full flight under a virtually clear blue 2017 New Year's Day sky.

Below: **BRIDGE 34** *Beatrice* has just passed the same location and will shortly be slowing to stop at Holywell Halt.

Above: **BRIDGE 34** is a farmer's access used by just sheep and cattle, but was in need of substantial repairs when the society took over, which is why its parapets are now in red brick. *Norman* powers away from beneath the bridge on the climb from Draughton on 18 April 2017.

HOLYWELL HALT

Before arriving at the Halt the train has to pass beneath the bridge that carries the busy A59 road over the line. The concrete-surrounded Armco arch, inserted to strengthen the bridge, can clearly be determined in this shot of the approaching No 22.

HOLYWELL HALT The new 'station' was built by volunteers and named after an old well. A picnic area has also been created. The cutting by the bridge is designated a 'Site of Scientific Interest' as there is visible evidence of the South Craven Fault in the rocky outcrop.

Below: **NR HOLYWELL HALT** Two years earlier the Bo'ness & Kinneil's 'D49/1' 4-4-0 No 246 *Morayshire* had travelled south of the border for the very first time, and a fine sight it made at the head of the 'Stately Trains' vintage set.

Above: **HOLYWELL HALT** The 2010 'Santa Specials' had the benefit of snow to create a wonderful Christmas card landscape. *Darfield* was the locomotive in charge.

Left: **HOLYWELL HALT** As the train leaves Holywell Halt bound for Embsay an old footbridge comes into view. This is a great vantage point for photography.

Left: **SKIBEDEN** Between the footbridge and Embsay station is Skibeden, in the shadow of former quarry workings. On a cold crisp winter's day, 5 December 2010, a Bolton Abbey-bound train leaves a steam trail in the cold still air in this view from Eastby Crags.

Below: **LOW LANE** is the location for this snowy springtime vista on 23 March 2008.

MIDLAND

On 17 August 2017 *Beatrice* was working the mid-week services and was photographed arriving at Embsay on a lovely summer's afternoon.

On 6 July 2018, following the official naming ceremony, *Illingworth/Mitchell* is seen departing from Embsay with the 'Stately Trains' Victorian London & South Western Railway 1st Open Royal Saloon No 17 and the Lancashire & Yorkshire Railway Directors Saloon in tow. *Courtesy of Andrew Rapacz*

BOW BRIDGE Most 'off-peak' services terminate at Embsay. However, in high season and at some special event weekends locomotives with trains from Bolton Abbey will pass through the station to run round at Bow Bridge loop just before the former junction with the Grassington branch. In this view over the village, Embsay station is just visible above and to the right of the farmhouse.

BOW BRIDGE In this 4 May 2015 view, visiting *Moorbarrow* has run round its goods train at Bow Bridge and is heading back to Embsay.

The future

THE N.E.R. 1903 ELECTRIC AUTOCAR In 1903, while steam powered most methods of transport and many factories around the country, the North Eastern Railway, looking at alternatives, designed and built a pair of 'autocars' that used a petrol engine to drive a dynamo to supply power to electric motors that drove the wheels. This was the world's first use of an internal combustion engine in a passenger-carrying rail vehicle, laying the foundation for most of the trains running today. Initially the autocars saw service around Hartlepool and Scarborough, later transferring to the Selby-Cawood branch line to work the passenger services there. Withdrawal came in 1930/31.

The body of No 3170 was sold to a North Yorkshire landowner, who converted it into a holiday home at Keldholme near Kirkbymoorside on the North Yorkshire Moors. Thankfully it was well protected from the weather and survived there until September 2003, when it was sold to carriage restorer Stephen Middleton (of 'Stately Trains'), who moved it to the Embsay & Bolton Abbey Railway.

Stephen Middleton and two colleagues placed the project in the care of a dedicated trust to attract funding for a full restoration. In October 2018 this restoration was completed sufficiently to allow this 'pioneer' to once again work passenger services for Trust members and invited guests. With final completion works to be carried out over the winter it should enter public service in the summer of 2019. *Courtesy of Andrew Rapacz*

THE N.E.R. 1903 ELECTRIC AUTOCAR TRUST

PLATFORMS 2 AND 3 AT BOLTON ABBEY: The society is aiming to complete the platforms at Bolton Abbey station, with an access footbridge and associated station buildings. Progress has already been made with the platform's construction.

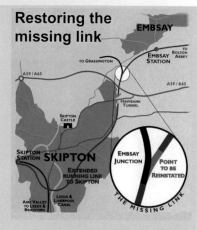

Restoring the missing link

Above: SKIPTON EXTENSION:
The society is also very excited by the prospect of running from Skipton through Embsay to Bolton Abbey! The track is already in situ (it is used by the quarry trains that serve Swinden Quarry) and the platforms still exist at Skipton station. Embsay junction would need to be reconnected, redevelopment work at Skipton station undertaken, and the railway would need to acquire suitable rolling stock and meet some legislative requirements before this can happen.

Right:: **EMBSAY JUNCTION** LNER 'K4' *The Great Marquess* is seen here at Embsay Junction in 1963 with 'The Dalesman Railtour', just before progressing up the Grassington branch (left). The site of Bow Bridge Loop is just behind the signal visible above the signal box in the photograph. *YDRMT Archive, Gavin Morrison*

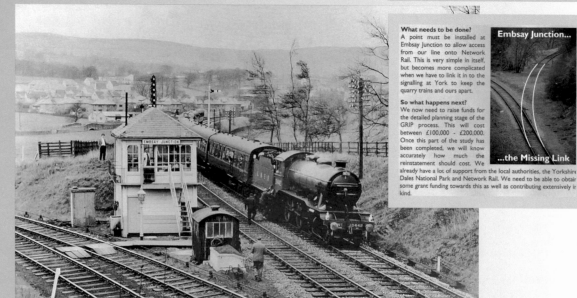

What needs to be done?
A point must be installed at Embsay Junction to allow access from our line onto Network Rail. This is very simple in itself, but becomes more complicated when we have to link it in to the signalling at York to keep the quarry trains and ours apart.

So what happens next?
We now need to raise funds for the detailed planning stage of the GRIP process. This will cost between £100,000 - £200,000. Once this part of the study has been completed, we will know accurately how much the reinstatement should cost. We already have a lot of support from the local authorities, the Yorkshire Dales National Park and Network Rail. We need to be able to obtain some grant funding towards this as well as contributing extensively in kind.

Embsay Junction...

...the Missing Link